Fun with PAPER

Clever Crafts

Annalees Lim

WINDMILL
BOOKS™
New York

Published in 2013 by Windmill Books, An Imprint of Rosen Publishing
29 East 21st Street, New York, NY 10010

Editor for Wayland: Victoria Brooker
US Editor: Sara Antill
Designer: Lisa Peacock
Photographer: Simon Pask
US Book Layout: Greg Tucker
Images used for creative graphics: Shutterstock
Cover picture: Thanks to Malachy Burke

Library of Congress Cataloging-in-Publication Data

Lim, Annalees.
 Fun with paper / by Annalees Lim.
     p. cm. — (Clever crafts)
 Includes index.
 ISBN 978-1-4777-0183-6 (library binding) — ISBN 978-1-4777-0194-2 (pbk.) —
 ISBN 978-1-4777-0195-9 (6-pack)
 1. Paper work—Juvenile literature. I. Title.
 TT870.L485 2013
 745.54—dc23

                                2012026226

Manufactured in the United States of America

CPSIA Compliance Information: Batch #BW13WM: For Further Information contact Windmill Books, New York, New York at 1-866-478-0556

Contents

Fun with Paper

You can find paper everywhere in different sizes, shapes, colors, and textures. From colored paper to newspaper, tissue paper to wrapping paper, paper can be found all around your home.

Transforming your piece of paper is easy. In this book, you will learn how to decorate paper using paints and coloring pens; join paper with glue, tape, and staples; and shape your paper by folding, tearing, and cutting.

Paper is the perfect material to be creative with. Once you learn the basics, there is no end to the paper crafts you can make. Try adapting the projects in this book using different designs, colors, or by adding glitter and sparkles.

Wrapping paper

Newspaper

Colored pencils

In this book, you will need:

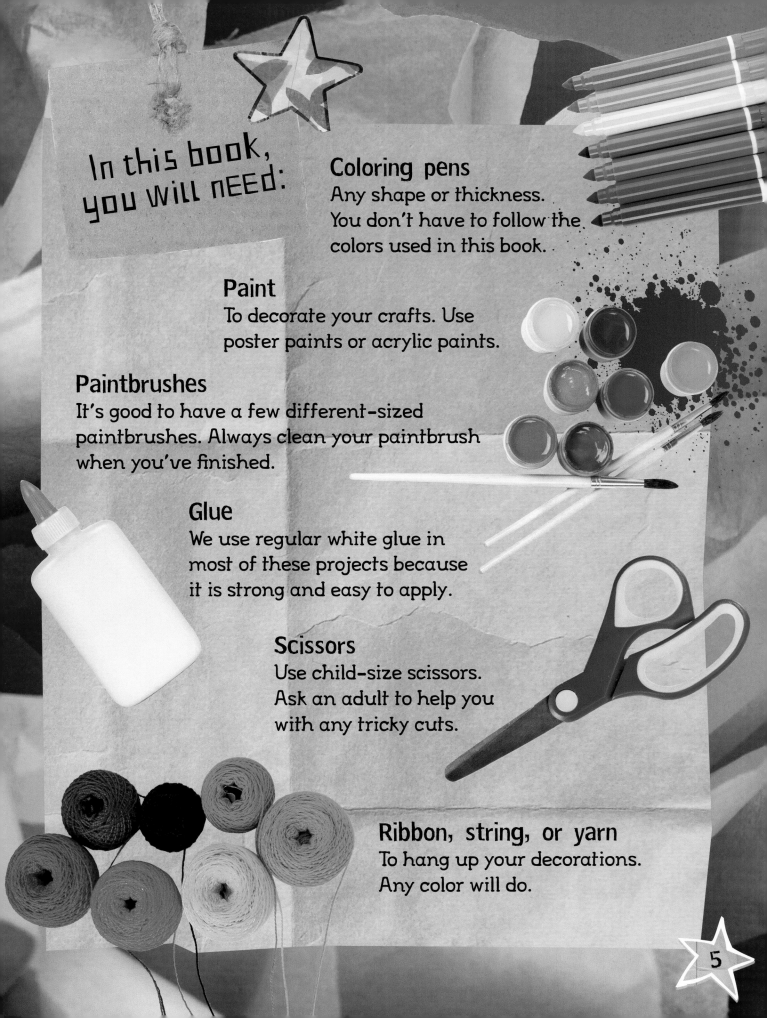

Coloring pens
Any shape or thickness. You don't have to follow the colors used in this book.

Paint
To decorate your crafts. Use poster paints or acrylic paints.

Paintbrushes
It's good to have a few different-sized paintbrushes. Always clean your paintbrush when you've finished.

Glue
We use regular white glue in most of these projects because it is strong and easy to apply.

Scissors
Use child-size scissors. Ask an adult to help you with any tricky cuts.

Ribbon, string, or yarn
To hang up your decorations. Any color will do.

Paper Pet Chains

You will need:

Piece of paper about 24 inches
(60 cm) long and 4 inches
(10 cm) wide
Ruler
Pencil
Scissors
Coloring pens
Scrap pieces of colored paper,
glitter, and glue to decorate

Decorate your room with these cute paper pals. You can use your own pet as inspiration, or dream up a new creature to hang on your walls.

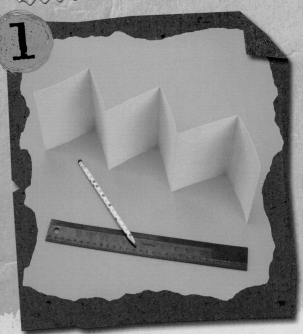

1

Fold the piece of paper backward and forward into an accordion shape, making sure that the folds are 4 inches (10 cm) wide.

2

Draw the picture of your pet on the top fold. The picture must touch both sides of the paper. This will make sure that all the pets are linked together.

Paper chains aren't just great for your bedroom, they are also a fantastic way to decorate a room for parties. Just draw a picture that matches the theme and cut out to create the perfect party paper chains.

4

Decorate each pet shape using your coloring pens, glitter, or scraps of paper. You can make each one the same, or all different.

3

Cut out the shape using scissors and open out.

Animal Masks

Go wild with this lion mask! But don't stop there. Why not make a happy hippo or an exotic bird of paradise?

You will need:

Orange and yellow paper plates
Scissors
A sharp pencil
Glue
Tissue paper
Coloring pens
Hole punch
String or elastic

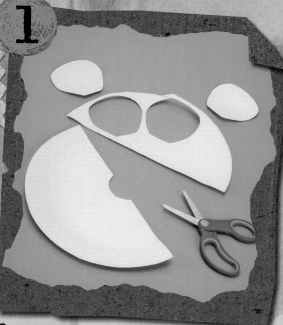

Cut the yellow plate in half. In one half, cut out a small semicircle shape in the middle of the flat side to fit around your nose. Use the other half to cut out two ears and a nose.

2

Use a pencil to mark where you would like the eye holes to be. Ask an adult to cut out the eye shapes.

3

Cut the orange plate into 8 segments. Glue these orange pieces around the yellow plate to make the mane. Then glue the yellow ears and nose on.

4

Cut slits into a length of tissue paper to make some extra mane. Glue this behind the paper mane. Draw around the edges with coloring pens to make the features stand out.

5

Use your hole punch to make holes at the side of the mask. Tie string or elastic on and it's ready to wear!

9

Accordion Butterflies

You will need:

Colored construction paper
Scissors
6 sheets of tissue paper
Stapler
Tape
Hole punch
Colored ribbon or string

Make fluttering butterflies, soaring birds, and other fun flying creatures to hang from your ceiling. We will be making a beautiful butterfly, but you can use the same technique to make any winged creature you can think of!

1 Draw the shape of a butterfly's body onto the colored construction paper and cut out.

2 Lay three pieces of tissue paper on top of each other and fold them backward and forward as if you were making a fan. Repeat with the other three pieces of tissue paper.

3

Cut the folded pieces of tissue paper in half to make 4 pieces. Make sure that two of the pieces are longer than the other two.

4

Fan out each tissue paper piece and staple in place on the construction paper butterfly body.

5

Cut out another piece of construction paper, slightly smaller than the butterfly body, and glue on top of the pink body. Make a hole in the top of the head using the hole punch. Tie some ribbon through the hole and hang your butterfly up.

Robot Weaving

Make a robot with a colorful circuit board tummy by weaving with colored pieces of paper. You can make your robots different shapes and sizes. Just use your imagination to create a fantastic team of robots.

You will need:

Gray construction paper
Black coloring pen
Scissors
Ruler
Colored paper cut into
0.5 inch (1 cm) wide strips

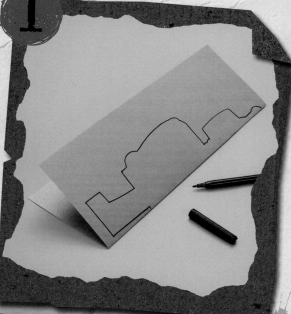

Fold the gray paper in half lengthwise and draw half a robot. Draw one leg, one arm, half a body, and half a head as shown above.

2

Cut out the shape of the robot and keep it folded in half.

3

Using your ruler, draw lines on the body of your robot that are about 0.5 inch (1 cm) apart. Cut along the lines.

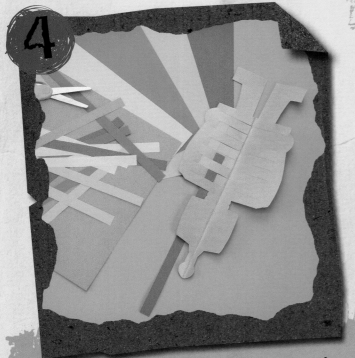

4

Open out the robot. Weave the colored strips of paper in and out of the slits you have cut. Switch from starting under to over for each slit.

5

Cut the ends of the colored paper strips so they don't show. Draw the details of your robot with the black coloring pen.

Mosaic Minibeasts

You will need:
Scraps of paper
Scissors
Ruler
Glue
White paper
Pencil
Black construction paper

You don't need to travel to ancient Rome to enjoy mosaics. Make your own using any paper you can find and cutting it into small squares. Recycle scraps of wrapping paper, old birthday cards, or magazines to create your minibeast masterpiece.

1

Cut the pieces of scrap paper into 1 inch (2.5 cm) wide strips, and then cut each strip into small squares that are roughly the same size.

2

Stick the squares of colored paper onto the white paper leaving a small gap between each square.

You can use your mosaic minibeasts to decorate almost anything. Stick them on notebooks, cards, or mount them in a frame.

4

Cut the shapes out. Repeat all the steps to make more mosaics for your minibeasts scene. You will need some leaves, a caterpillar, a butterfly, and a dragonfly. Stick all of these onto the black piece of construction paper.

3

Make a stencil by drawing a flower shape on a piece of paper. Cut it out and draw around it two times on the mosaic.

15

Stapled Paper Hearts

These lovely decorations are perfect to make and hang in your window. You could use sparkly paper to make them really catch the light.

Try using smaller pieces of paper to make smaller hearts. They are perfect to use as fancy gift tags.

You will need:
Colored paper
Scissors
Stapler
Yarn or string
Tape

1

Cut 4 strips of paper the same width but different lengths. Staple them together at one end. Do this again to make two bundles of paper.

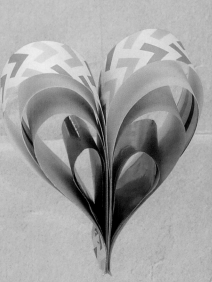

2

Staple both of the paper bundles together. Make sure the shortest pieces are on the outside.

3

Fold the strips of paper on one side halfway down toward the stapled end of the bundles. Line the edges up and staple the strips to the bundle.

4

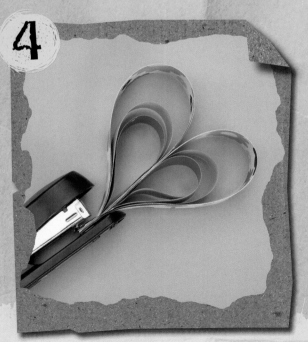

Repeat on the other side to make the heart shape and staple to fix in place.

5

Make three hearts in total. Attach a short piece of yarn or string to the top of each heart with tape. Stick them together to make a string of hearts, ready to hang.

Shoe Box Swamp

You will need:
The base of an old shoe box
Paint
Paintbrush
Colored construction paper
Scissors
Black coloring pen
Glue

Transform an old shoe box into a super swamp filled with overhanging trees, lily pads, and a hopping frog.

1

Paint your shoe box. Paint green on the bottom and blue on the top, sides, and outside.

2

Using different shades of green paper, cut out a wavy shape for some hills and a spiky shape for the grass.

3

Using other colored paper, cut out a pond, lily pads, clouds, trees, reeds, and flowers.

Try creating different scenes, such as outer space, filled with planets, stars, and zooming rockets!

4

Glue the pond, hills, and clouds in first. Then stick the trees on the side.

5

Cut out a shape of a frog from some green paper. Draw the frog's features using a black coloring pen. Add the frog to your scene along with any other small details such as flowers and reeds. Your scene is complete!

Fruity Fridge Magnets

Foil is a great material to mold into any shape. Make any fridge magnets you like. Why not try some letters or numbers?

Decorate the outside of your fridge with these fun food magnets! Use them to attach handy notes to the fridge or to display pieces of art you have just made.

You will need:
Foil
Tissue paper
Glue
Paintbrush
Black coloring pen
Magnets
Double-sided tape

1

Scrunch up a piece of tin foil about 20 inches (50 cm) long and shape it into a strawberry shape, which is similar to a heart shape.

Cover the whole shape in small pieces of red tissue paper using glue. Leave to dry in a warm space.

Draw some seeds onto the strawberry using the black coloring pen.

Cut five leaf shapes with long stems out of green tissue paper. Twist them together and glue them on top of the strawberry.

Using double-sided tape or glue, stick a magnet to the back of the strawberry. When it is dry you can stick it to a fridge or any metal surface.

Tissue Paper Sunlight Catchers

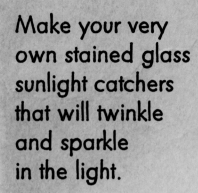

Make your very own stained glass sunlight catchers that will twinkle and sparkle in the light.

You will need:

Sheet of plastic
Tissue paper
Glue
Black coloring pen
Scissors
Thread

1

Cut lots of different shapes out of tissue paper, or rip some into small squares.

2

Glue them onto a sheet of plastic in a random pattern using the glue. Leave to dry in a warm place until completely dry. This could take up to 24 hours.

3

Make a template of a star. Draw around this template onto your tissue paper pattern using a black coloring pen.

4

Cut out all your shapes. You can cut out just stars, or you could cut out different shapes, too.

5

Stick a piece of thread on top of the stars using tape and hang up your sunlight catcher!

23

Glossary

accordion (uh-KOR-dee-un) A shape made by folding paper backward and forward.

magnet (MAG-net) A metal material that sticks to other metal materials.

mane (MAYN) The long hair around a lion's neck.

masterpiece (MAS-tur-pees) A fantastic piece of artwork.

minibeast (MIH-nee-beest) A small animal such as a bee, ladybug, beetle, or spider.

mosaic (moh-ZAY-ik) A picture made from lots of smaller pieces of paper, tiles, or glass.

paper chain (PAY-per CHAYN) A decoration made by joining pieces of paper together.

swamp (SWOMP) A very muddy pond or lake.

template (TEM-plut) A shape you can draw around again and again to make the same shape.

tissue paper (TIH-shoo PAY-per) Very thin paper often used as wrapping paper.

Index

Websites

For web resources related to the subject of this book, go to:
www.windmillbooks.com/weblinks
and select this book's title.